GAMES (& other stuff) FOR GROUP

·BOOK 2·

by Chris Cavert & Friends

Published by:

Wood & Barnes Publishing
2717 NW 50th
Oklahoma City, OK 73112
(405) 942-6812

Cover Art by Chris Cavert.
Copyediting & Design by Ramona Cunningham

Printed in the United States of America
Oklahoma City, Oklahoma
ISBN # 1-885473-21-4

To order copies of this book, please call:
Jean Barnes Books
800-678-0621

YOU TEAR ME UP

Thanks to Karl Rohnke, *Bottomless Bag Again*

NEEDS: You will need a blank piece of 8 1/2" x 11" paper for each participant. Sometimes I will do this activity after *Dark Doodling* and use the piece of paper they drew on (if they don't want to keep their drawing).

PROCEDURE: Hand each participant a sheet of paper. Ask them to work on their own - "Even though there are others around you, please do your own work." Tell the participants that they are not allowed to ask or answer any questions during the activity, but they can talk freely among themselves. When everyone is ready, give the following directions, in order, repeating each direction twice, giving the next direction only when each participant has completed the stated direction (don't move on until everyone is ready).

1. Fold the paper in half and tear off the bottom left hand corner. Save this corner.
2. Fold the paper in half again and tear off the upper right hand corner. Save this corner.
3. Fold the paper in half again and tear off the upper left hand corner. Save this corner.

When every participant is finished, open up the papers and compare the results. Snowflakes.

POSSIBLE OBJECTIVES:
- Interpretation of ambiguous directions through choices.
- Communicating understanding before starting a task.
- It's not easy giving directions.

(others)
-
-

Note: I like to use this activity with a new group so I can let them know that I'm not always going to communicate clearly to them. It will be very important to ask questions if there is confusion.

OBSERVATIONS/QUESTIONS:
- Are any of the snowflakes the same? Why?
- Did anyone ask questions during the activity? What were the directions?

- Was it frustrating, not to be able to ask questions?
- Were you able to do your own work?
- Did anyone look at another person's work for ideas?
- What do you think about getting ideas from someone else? Copying?
- Has there ever been a time when you gave someone directions and they didn't do what you expected them to do?
- How can we eliminate some of the confusion about following directions?
- How many of you have a hard time asking questions? Why?

(others) •

•

VARIATIONS:

- Feel free to ask your own directions. Keep in mind that if you fold an 8 1/2" x 11" sheet of paper more than three times it is very difficult to tear.
- Karl suggests to blindfold participants or have them close their eyes during the activity. This works well if you don't want to open the doors that keeping your eyes open open.
- Another option along the same line is to ask participants to draw shapes on their paper following your instructions. For example: Draw a small circle. Draw a square so the bottom right hand corner touches the circle. Put a diamond in the square, and so on. This could be done before the Dark Doodles activity and compare the results.

OTHER IDEAS:

NEEDS: You will not need any formal props for this one, just bodies.

PROCEDURE: This is a name game activity that I adapted from my friend Karl's *FUNN Stuff* volume one. I most often use it with a new group, but have found it just as fun with a group that has been together for a while (see the variations for ideas).

Sitting around in a circle is the best way to play. If you are using chairs, have one extra chair in the circle for movement (you'll see).

There are three motions in this game. These motions will always be done in the same order. The first motion is an open hand on top of the head. The open fingers of the hand can either be pointing to the left or to the right - using the right arm, the fingers will be pointing to the left, left arm fingers pointing to the right. The second motion is the same as the first, however, it is done on the chest area. The third motion is a straight arm out in front of the player, hand open, pointing to another player across the circle.

Here's how it works. You start the game with the first motion. Put your right hand on your head with your fingers pointing left. John happens to be on your left. You say, "John." So now it's John's turn. John has a choice. Using the second move, he can either point right (back to you) or left. He uses his right arm and placing his hand on his chest with his fingers pointing left to Scott, says, "Scott." Scott uses the third move pointing straight out to a player across the circle, "Ron." Ron uses the first move to continue the action. Using the moves in order, continue with the game.

The ultra idea here is to keep the game going, lively, keep it snappy, get the lead out, and so on. If it drags it might be a drag. So it is up to you to keep the spark. With this in mind, make sure to go around the circle a couple of times reviewing names before you start. Or, try another activity like, *Interviews*, before embarking on this one.

As the sparks are flying mistakes might happen. If a mistake is made, the player who made the mistake must move to an open space in the circle and start the game over with the first move.

POSSIBLE **O**BJECTIVES:
- Learning names.
- Dealing with mistakes.

•Physical and mental interaction.

(others)   •

            •

Note: Let the group establish the tolerance level for mistakes. In the beginning it might be acceptable to cut a little slack for learning. As the games go on the skill will increase and the tolerance may lower. So much to talk about, so little time.

I may be preaching to the choir here but, please make sure the group is laughing with and not at each other. It just seems to be more fun that way.

OBSERVATIONS/**Q**UESTIONS:

•Who is able to pick up names? Who is not? Why?
•What feelings did you have during the activity?
•How did you feel when you made a mistake? Where does that come from?
•Was anyone uncomfortable during the game? At what time?
•Was anyone embarrassed? Why?
•What was difficult about the activity?
•Can anyone go around the circle and say every person's name?

(others)   •

            •

VARIATIONS:

•If your group has been together for some time, use nicknames or favorite foods instead of names (or any other trait for that matter).
•Set up the game, "to be continued...." Any time you're in a circle and you want to charge things up slap your hand on your head and shout, "John." And the game is on.

OTHER **I**DEAS:

—DARK DOODLING————————————

NEEDS: You will need one blank piece of 8 1/2" x 11" paper and one pencil for each participant. Blindfolds for each person would be good if there might be an issue of keeping the eyes closed (and that's always something to talk about). I also recommend a hard surface to write on - tables are ideal, a hard floor is the next best.

PROCEDURE: Before you get started, make sure you discuss the blindfolded/being blind issue (if needed). To get the full experience of this activity, it is best to keep the eyes shut. (If the drawings are too good, then you might inquire if some peeking was going on!?)

When everyone has their supplies and the "lights are out," give the following instructions. (Feel free to add or delete any instructions, but be sure to give a bit of time for each instruction to be carried out.)

1 Start with your paper sideways for our trip to the Rockies and draw some mountains across the horizon.

2. Now draw a nice cool refreshing lake in the valley below the mountains.

3. Since it hasn't warmed up yet, let's put some snowcaps on the mountains.

4. Now we'll need some fish in the lake so we can catch some dinner.

5. Since it is around dinner time, draw the sun going down behind the mountains.

6. We'll need to set up our tent before it gets dark. Let's put it next to the lake.

7. The clouds seem to be rolling in. Let's put a few clouds in the sky.

8. It's getting to be a bit cooler now that the sun is going down, let's build a fire ring and a fire close to the tent - be careful, not too close.

9. The elk are coming out to graze. Draw some elk along the sides of the mountains.

10. One more thing. It would be nice if we had some trees to block that cool wind coming in. Draw two trees near the lake.

When all the participants have finished, ask them to take off their blindfolds or open their eyes. A masterpiece!

POSSIBLE OBJECTIVES:
- Break the ice with a fun and silly activity.
- Assess frustration levels.

(others) •

•

Note: The outcome of this activity usually produces grand laughter. Laughter is the best ice-breaker there is. Use the questions below to promote some discussion.

Be careful however. I have had instances where this activity induced some anger. The underlying cause was often the lack of perfection in the artwork (and the history behind that). Watch out for the criticism also. All are good things to talk about.

OBSERVATIONS/QUESTIONS:
- What were some of the feelings that were coming up for you during the activity?
- When have you had these same feelings in the past?
- Was there any point during the drawing when you gave up? Why?
- Was there any point during the activity when you just thought it was silly? Why?
- What comments were made during the activity?
- Did anyone peek? Why?
- What do you think the lesson of this drawing might be?

(others) •

•

VARIATIONS:

OTHER IDEAS:

MY PERSONAL STRENGTHS SHEET

Thanks to Jack Canfield and Self-Esteem Seminars

NEEDS: You will want a copy of, *My Personal Strengths Sheet,* and a pencil for each person in your group.

PROCEDURE: I like to use this checklist to find out a little more about the personalities within my groups. You will have to decide the best way to use this sheet for your group. I have spent several sessions going through this sheet and have used it every once in a while - working on just "A's" one session, then the "B's" in another, and so on.

POSSIBLE OBJECTIVES:
- Learning more about group members.
- Identify qualities of self and others.
- Positive reinforcement.

(others)
-
-

Note: Don't forget to build in time for defining some of these qualities. Definitions might also vary. So when you discuss the qualities, find out what each person believes that quality to be.

OBSERVATIONS/QUESTIONS:
- Was is difficult to "rate" yourself?
- Do you express the traits that you checked off?
- Would other people make a different check sheet for you?
- Was there any surprise over other group members' strengths?
- What strengths would you add to the sheet?
- (Develop your own questions from the traits given)

(others)
-
-

VARIATIONS:
- Have the group do a sheet for you. You could leave the room for a short time so they could talk about the sheet and fill it in. I have found this to be a great way to get feedback from my group.
- This could take a lot of time, but what about group members filling out sheets for other group members? Maybe do a sheet together for someone who is going to transition out of the group.

OTHER IDEAS FOR MY PERSONAL STRENGTHS SHEET:

MY PERSONAL STRENGTHS SHEET

Place a check mark next to each strength that you think you have. You might also have another group member go over the list and tell you which ones they think you have. Sometimes other people see our strengths more than we do.

- [ ] able to give orders
- [ ] able to take orders
- [ ] able to take care of self
- [ ] accepts advice
- [ ] admires others
- [ ] affectionate
- [ ] alive
- [ ] appreciative
- [ ] articulate
- [ ] artistic
- [ ] assertive
- [ ] athletic
- [ ] attractive

- [ ] bright
- [ ] brave
- [ ] businesslike

- [ ] calm
- [ ] can be firm if necessary
- [ ] caring
- [ ] clean
- [ ] committed
- [ ] common sense
- [ ] communicates well
- [ ] compassionate
- [ ] considerate
- [ ] cooperative
- [ ] courteous
- [ ] creative

- [ ] daring
- [ ] dedicated
- [ ] dependable
- [ ] diligent
- [ ] disciplined

- [ ] does what needs to be done
- [ ] doesn't give up

- [ ] eager to get along with others
- [ ] eager to please
- [ ] effective
- [ ] efficient
- [ ] elegant
- [ ] encourages others
- [ ] enjoys taking care of others

- [ ] fair
- [ ] feeling
- [ ] forceful
- [ ] frank and honest
- [ ] friendly
- [ ] funny

- [ ] generous
- [ ] gets along with others
- [ ] gets things done
- [ ] gives a lot
- [ ] goal setter
- [ ] good cook
- [ ] good dancer
- [ ] good friend
- [ ] good leader
- [ ] good listener
- [ ] good-looking
- [ ] good manners
- [ ] good neighbor
- [ ] good parent
- [ ] good singer
- [ ] good with details
- [ ] good with hands

- [ ] good with words
- [ ] graceful
- [ ] grateful

- [ ] happy
- [ ] hard worker
- [ ] healthy
- [ ] helpful
- [ ] honest
- [ ] humorous

- [ ] independent
- [ ] inspiring
- [ ] intelligent

- [ ] joyful

- [ ] keeps agreements
- [ ] kind and reassuring

- [ ] leadership
- [ ] likes responsibility
- [ ] lots of friends
- [ ] lovable
- [ ] loving
- [ ] loyal

- [ ] makes a difference
- [ ] makes a good impression
- [ ] mathematical
- [ ] mechanical
- [ ] motivates others
- [ ] musical

- [ ] never gives up

- [ ] observant
- [ ] often admired
- [ ] orderly
- [ ] organized

- [ ] on time
- [ ] open

- [ ] patient
- [ ] peaceful
- [ ] physically fit
- [ ] pleasant
- [ ] positive attitude

- [ ] quick learner

- [ ] religious
- [ ] resilient
- [ ] respectful of authority
- [ ] respected by others
- [ ] responsible
- [ ] risk taker

- [ ] self-reliant
- [ ] self-confident
- [ ] self-respecting
- [ ] sense of humor
- [ ] sensitive
- [ ] speaks several languages
- [ ] spiritual
- [ ] spontaneous
- [ ] straightforward and direct
- [ ] strong

- [ ] team player
- [ ] tolerant
- [ ] trusting
- [ ] truthful
- [ ] understanding
- [ ] unselfish

- [ ] visionary

- [ ] warm
- [ ] well-dressed

OODLES OF DOODLES

Thanks to Jim Cain

NEEDS: *One Doodles* handout and a pencil for each participant and one set of "Evaluating the Results" to read from.

PROCEDURE: Hand out a *Doodles* sheet and a pencil to everyone. Have the participants draw, sketch, write, doodle or scribble something in each of the eight squares.

After all the participants have finished doodling, Jim suggests, "Have each member of the group [take turns reading] one of the subjects. The question at the end of each paragraph can be answered by the reader and then by the other members of the group. Take time for participants to share their stories and experiences surrounding each subject."

POSSIBLE **O**BJECTIVES:
- Getting to know more about each other.
- Sharing and speaking with the group.

(others)
-
-

Note: Jim says that the information on the evaluation sheet, "has little or no scientific basis. The real purpose of this exercise [information] is more in the conversation surrounding the evaluation of your doodles than the actual evaluation. In other words, have fun, and don't take answers (or yourself) too seriously."

OBSERVATIONS/**Q**UESTIONS:
- Does everyone draw in all the squares?
- How do your drawings compare to the suggested evaluation?
- Do you agree with what is suggested?
- Is everyone sharing in the conversation? How can you pull others in?
- What did you learn about yourself?
- How are you like some of the others in the group?
- How are you different from others in the group?

(others)
-
-

adapted from Cain, Jim & Jolliff, Barry, *Teamwork & Teamplay*, 1998, Kendall/Hunt Publishing Company

VARIATIONS:

• This activity could take a long time to complete. You may want to break it up into sets of three or even just one square. Enlarge the squares so the participants have more area to doodle.

OTHER **I**DEAS:

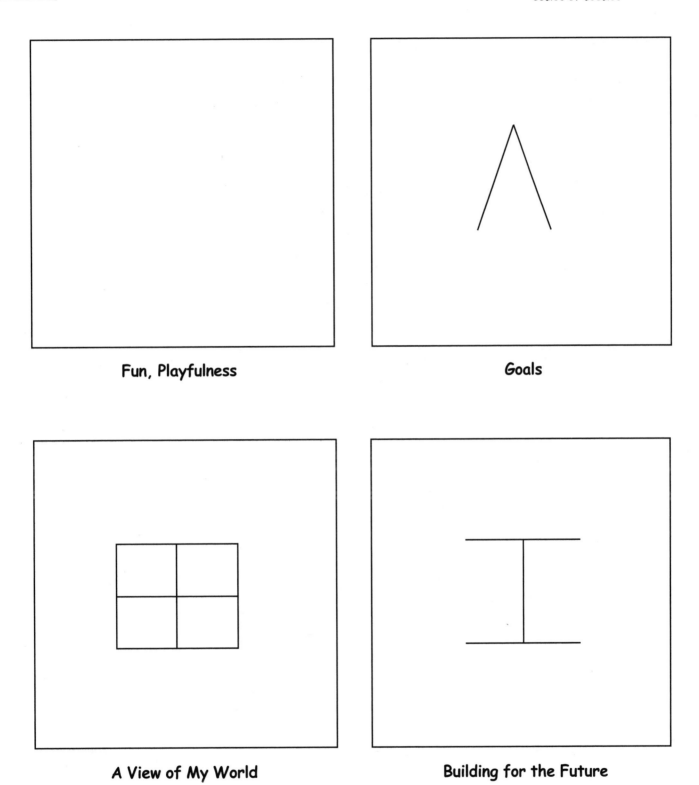

Fun, Playfulness

Goals

A View of My World

Building for the Future

INSTRUCTIONS: Draw, scribble, write, doodle or sketch something in each of the four squares.

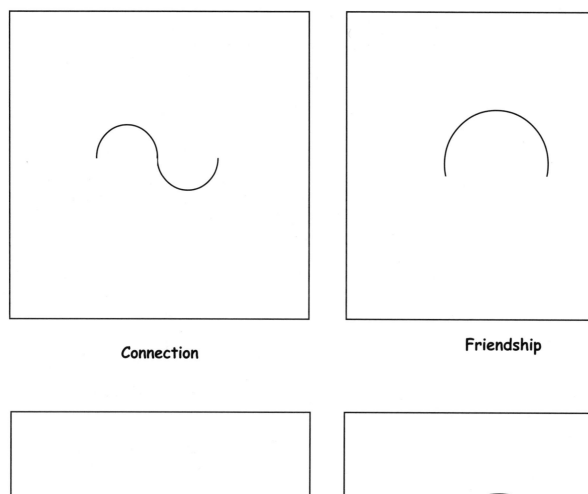

Connection

Friendship

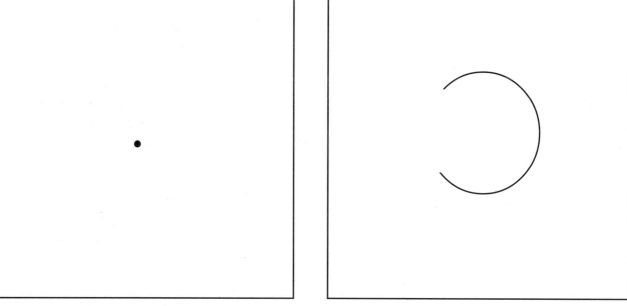

Imagination

Creativity

INSTRUCTIONS: Draw, scribble, write, doodle or sketch something in each of the four squares.

OODLES OF DOODLES - Evaluating the Results

The following information has little or no scientific basis. The real purpose of this exercise is more in the conversation surrounding the evaluation of your doodles than in the actual evaluation. In other words, have fun and don't take the answers (or yourself) too seriously.

INSTRUCTIONS:

Have each member of the group read one of the following subjects. The question at the end of each paragraph can be answered by the reader and then by the other members of the group. Take time for participants to share their personal stories and experiences surrounding each subject.

Connection - If you drew an elephant or roller coaster, you have a high level of creativity. If you drew sunglasses or a face, you have creative friends. Question: Do you like to create things by yourself or with other people?

Friendship - If you used this space to draw a sunset, you have close friends. If you drew a face or baseball cap, you have a good friend. If you drew a wheel or pizza, you like to go places with your friends. Question: What do you and your friends like to do together?

Imagination - If you made a face, this is your own self-image! If you made many more dots, you are orderly and possibly keep your room clean. Question: Have you ever invented a better way to do something?

Creativity - If you finish the circle, draw a wheel, CD, or pizza, you have average creativity. If you draw outside the circle, you have high creativity. Question: Which of the following would you rather do - paint a picture?...color with crayons?...make something with blocks?...write your own book?

Goals - If you drew mountains or volcanoes, you have high goals. If you drew an upside-down ice cream cone, you are mixed up about where to go. If you drew a railroad track or road vanishing in the distance, you are ready to travel! Question: Where do you want to go in life?

A View of Your World - If you drew a window with curtains, you like your home. If you drew a map, you want to travel far and wide. If you drew a present or boxes, you like your family and friends. Question: What can you see from your bedroom window?

Fun, Playfulness - If you color in the shape, you like to add color to your world. If you add more scribbles to the block, you like to have lots of fun. Question: What's something you like to do that is really fun?

Building for the Future - Whatever you drew in this block shows what you want to build. If you drew a book, magazine or newspaper, you want to use words to build a better world. If you drew a spool, I-beam or geometric shape, you like to build things. Question: What is the coolest thing you have ever made?

— COUNT OFF —————————

Thanks to Karl Rohnke, *Bottomless Bag Again*

NEEDS: Only patience.

PROCEDURE: This activity is one of those easy to learn, challenging to accomplish tasks. It could be over in a matter of seconds, or not!?

Lets say you have 12 people in your group. Ask them to count up to 12 (starting with one), without any pre-planning who will say which number, and try to do this without having two (or more) people saying the same number simultaneously. Here are some other provisos to make it interesting.

1   No verbal or visual signals are allowed during play (I like to do this one with eyes closed).

2   No circular number pattern may be established - you can't just go around the circle 1, 2, 3, 4, ... no fun!

Anyone can begin the game saying, "One." If at any point in the game one number is called out by two or more players, the game starts over with, "One." I have found adding an obnoxious, "BUZZZZZZZZ" sound (from a facilitator/ judge type), when a mistake is made, helps to indicate starting over.

POSSIBLE **O**BJECTIVES:
> • Assessment of persistence levels.
> • Observation of frustration levels.
> • Group challenge - success/failure responses.
> • Who is having fun and who is not?

(others)   •

  •

Note: The biggest issue I have run into with this one is when to stop. I have played one game with some groups for more than 10 minutes. I let it go that long because all the group members, at the time, were very committed to the process. This does not happen very often.

Some of my most powerful processing sessions evolved after I stopped the game without making it to 12. There are so many issues around success and winning that I believe to eliminate them would change the world - so good luck! And that issue about stopping without a committed effort - that's another story. So it's in your hands. To stop or not to stop, that is *really* the question.

OBSERVATIONS/**Q**UESTIONS:
> • What were your/the initial reactions to the game?
> • How soon did the group start to get frustrated?
> • Is success possible? What does it take?
> • How quickly do you achieve success?
> • What hindered success?
> • What other feelings were present during the game?
> • Who wanted to give up? Keep going? Why?
> • Why did we have to stop before we completed?
> • Were we successful? In what ways?

(others)   •
>   •

VARIATIONS:
> • Sometimes I like to "count down" with the group: 12, 11, (you get the idea).
> • When I do assertiveness training, I will have group members close their eyes and instead of counting, slap their hand on the table. I count down quietly as I'm watching. Any two slaps at the same time elicits a loud "BUZZZZZZZZ" and the game starts over.
> • You can call out fruit until everyone has gone - anything will work.

OTHER **I**DEAS:

NEEDS: You will not need any formal props for this one.

PROCEDURE: This activity is one of those you can do just hanging out anywhere. One person in the group will tell three stories, about him or herself, to the rest of the group. Two stories will be true about the storyteller and one story will not be true. Then each person in the group is allowed to ask one question to the story teller that is related to any one of the stories (except, "is that true?")

After each person has had a chance to ask a question (they can pass also - not ask a question), then they will vote. Each player will cast a vote for which story they think is the fable. Once all the votes are in, the storyteller reveals the true fable (can there be a true fable?)

POSSIBLE **O**BJECTIVES:
  • Getting to know more about group members.
  • Speaking in front of the group.
  (others) •
  •

Note: Some groups may struggle with the fable part of this activity. To help out the process I will tell my group that it is okay to tell a story that happened to someone else. If Bob uses his name in Bill's story then it's a fable for Bob but not for Bill. Whatever works!

Word of warning. Make sure you emphasize the part about, "short story." I ask that each story be no longer than one minute - give or take a second or two.

OBSERVATIONS/**Q**UESTIONS:
  • Who is really listening during the stories? Who is distracting?
  • Did anyone feel uncomfortable telling this group their stories? Why?
  • What was the most difficult part of this activity?
  (others) •
  •

Most of the questions I use stem from the true stories that are told. It's a great way to open other doors. Even the fables are fun to explore.

VARIATIONS:
- Have each person tell just one story. Vote around to see if it's true or not. If there's time, talk about the story.

OTHER **I**DEAS:

NEEDS: You will want at least two sets of two different objects - that is, two tennis balls and two wads of white paper or something like that. Make sure it's small enough to hold in one hand and that it's soft enough to bump into face parts and not hurt anything (a hammer would not be a good idea for this one - even though we might think so sometimes). If your group is larger than 12, you might want to add another object to each set - that would be two sets of three similar objects (call me if this doesn't make sense).

PROCEDURE: You can do this activity standing in a close circle or sitting in a close circle of chairs. Whatever is most comfortable for the group.

An important factor in this one is an even number of players. (To play or not to play, will be your question.) Choose a player to start and <u>hand</u> (this should not be an air-born toss) that person a tennis ball (using props mentioned above). The starter will <u>hand-off</u> the ball to the player two over to his/her right after saying, "Watch it" (WITH GUSTO) to the player directly to his/her right. The directly right person should duck to avoid the hand-off overhead (the best action for this game is ducking - if players just hand-off in front of the participant next to them we lose the fun). This action goes around the circle until the ball returns to the starter.

Now, that directly right person that ducked first, given a wad of paper, says, "WATCH IT" to the "next directly right," person who ducks to avoid the overhead hand-off. This action goes around to the first person who handed off the wad. (Half the group passed around the tennis ball, the other half the wad of paper.) Now for the fun. Start the tennis ball, let it get two players down, then start the wad. And don't stop at the first person who started the game, just keep handing. You'll see how the mental and the physical work together (or not together - I'm still ducking when I'm supposed to be handing - crazy).

Add in more tennis balls and wads for some real chaos. Don't forget - STOP WHILE IT'S STILL FUN.

POSSIBLE **O**BJECTIVES:
- Composure in the midst of chaos.
- Opening up with the group.
- How chaos affects our attention level.

(others) ·

·

31

Note: I don't know if I made this up, but I'll say so until I find out that I didn't. "Watch It," has turned out to be a mental as well as a physical warm-up. I like to use this one to get some laughter going - if you can't get the group to laugh during this one, you will need to back up a few issues I'm afraid.

The most important safety concern in this game is getting "bopped" with an object. And for some groups, getting bopped leads to more bops. So make sure your group is ready for this activity, and stress the importance of handing-off the object <u>after</u> the person next to them ducks.

I also really like to stress the "WATCH IT" in a loud, forceful voice. This is especially true for the quieter participants and the girls that I have worked with on assertiveness.

OBSERVATIONS/**Q**UESTIONS:
- Who got involved, got into, really participated, in the game?
- Who didn't get involved? What issues are around not getting involved?
- Did anyone get confused? At what point?
- Who can explain what chaos is?
- What sort of chaos is going on in your life?
- How does the chaos in your life affect you inside?
- In what ways can we help ourselves deal with chaos?

(others)
-
-

VARIATIONS:

OTHER **I**DEAS:

NEEDS: You will need some paper and a pencil for each participant. I like to use 5" x 7" index cards so I can use them for, *Communication Walk* later on.

PROCEDURE: This one is really straightforward. Hand out four to six index cards to each participant in the group. Have them write a problem they might be facing in their lives, or for that matter any problem they might be aware of, on one card. Have them put a big "P" on this card. Then have them write a possible solution to that problem on another card. Indicate this card with a large "S". Initially, make sure the cards stay in order for the first round.

If time allows, I like to start out by writing problem cards. Then I present the problems to the group and brainstorm possible solutions. Many of my past participants can rattle off many problems but lack appropriate solutions to them.

When all of the players have completed at least one set of cards, go around and read the cards one at a time. State the problem and then the solution. If time allows, discuss the cards with the group.

At some point you'll want to try the Mix-and-Match part of the game. Mix all the problems up in one pile and the solutions in another. Then pick a problem and read it. Now pick out a solution. Some of the solutions may be quite funny in comparison to the problem, others might even be a viable option to the problem.

POSSIBLE **O**BJECTIVES:

- Develop steps to problem solving.
- Explore appropriate solutions to various problems.
- Group sharing.

(others)
-
-

Note: This activity can be used over several sessions. If you don't get to the Mix-and-Match right away make sure to end your P.S. sessions with something positive so the group will want to continue this activity in the future.

Try to encourage creative answers. If someone writes, "I have a problem swearing too much," and gives a solution of, "Don't swear," there is nothing in the solution that will modify the behavior. A modifying solution might be, "Give a quarter to the spring party jar every time I swear."

I have also had success using the acronym P.S. as a signal for someone to look for a solution to a problem they might be getting into at the time - a verbal cue so to speak.

OBSERVATIONS/**Q**UESTIONS:
- What seems to be harder to think of, problems or solutions?
- Did anyone contribute the same problem as another person?
- Has anyone ever tried any of the solutions given? How did they work?
- Why do you think there are so many problems in our lives?
- What can we do to eliminate some of the problems we have?
- Are you able to recognize your own problems?
- How do you react when someone else points out a problem you are having?
- Are you able to try another person's solution to a problem you might be having?

(others)·
- ·

VARIATIONS:
- Save the cards for the activity *Communication Walk* listed in this book.
- Carry around the solution cards. When a problem crops up, pick a card to see what happens.
- Another fun card resource I like to use for problem solving is the *"Creative Whack Pack,"* by Roger von Oech. The pack includes 64 cards consisting of different problem solving strategies and ideas. You can find the pack at most of your local book stores.

OTHER **I**DEAS:

MIX & MATCH

Thanks to Andy via Melanie via Mark

NEEDS: You will need one envelope for every two participants in your group and a bunch of Mix-and-Match sentences. (See Procedure.)

PROCEDURE: There is a little preparation involved in this one. You will want to choose some sentences to work with. These sentences can be anything from funny to serious. If you just want to break the ice with your group, make up some silly ones. If you want to talk about certain issues, make up some questions that will help you initiate your goal. Along with your thought process keep this in mind - each word of the sentence will need to be on a separate piece of paper that will fit within an envelope along with some other words. So, you can write sentences out, one word at a time, on note cards or type out the sentences, enlarge them a bit so they are easier to work with, then cut the words out. I have found when working this activity with partners, five or six words per envelope is a good number.

Now, how to play. Let's say you have 12 participants in your group. You chose six sentences to use (one sentence for each pair) - 30 words in all. You cut all the words out and mixed them up, then place a mixture of words in six different envelopes with five words in each one. When your group is together and you are all ready to play, pair up participants. Hand each pair an envelope. The small group objective of each pair is to end up with a sentence, that makes sense, laid out in front of them. The large group objective is for all teams to have sentences that make sense with no words left over. You may also impose the objective that all sentences must match the sentences that you started with. (We never impose objectives on our groups do we?) To make this all work, the pairs will have to communicate and trade words with each other, as they mix and match to make sentences.

Once you have reached any or all of the goals you can discuss the process, discuss the sentences, or both.

POSSIBLE OBJECTIVES:
- Communicating needs.
- Negotiational cooperation.
- Partner and group interaction.

(others)
-
-

Note: There is an assumption made that your group members will know how to create a proper sentence. This is one of the reasons I like to do this one in pairs. There are better odds that one out of the two should be able to create a sentence. Not much else you need to know for this one. I can say this activity is one of my all-time favorites to watch.

OBSERVATIONS/**Q**UESTIONS:

- Who is most involved? Who is not? Why?
- What sort of communication is being used? Positive? Negative?
- Does any leadership emerge?
- What is negotiation? How can it be helpful to us?
- How are the partners interacting with each other? With the group?
- Did anyone ask for help in any way?
- Did the group pool words together or did partners keep words to themselves?
- Who was successful?
- Is there a way to be more successful in the future?

(others)
-
-

VARIATIONS:

- Check out the *Metaphors* section for some enlightening sentences - a great deal of interesting topics to choose from.
- If you have more time, make up an envelope for each participant in your group.
- What if you had eight small groups and only six sentences. You can change the rules around a bit to see what happens.
- I like to do silly sentences one session, then play again later down the road with the more serious ones.
- Try cutting out lines of a poem and having the entire group put the poem back together. My favorite is Foster W. Cline's, *Rules for Being Human*.

OTHER **I**DEAS:

NEEDS: Provide two paper clips for each pair of players in your group. I like to start out with the big ones and have the smaller ones available for an added challenge.

PROCEDURE: First we will need to establish some terminology. Look at a paper clip. There are three bends in a regular clip - two bends near one end and one bend at the other. Look at the end with the two bends. There is an outside bend and an inside bend (the inside bend being the one "inside" the clip. Imagine a paper clip without an inside bend. Would it be able to clip? Sorry I get sidetracked easily). The inside bend is the key to setting up.

Take two paper clips and attach them together so the two "inside" bends are interlocked. If you were to pull the clips apart by the single bend ends, only the inside bends will be touching (an initiative in itself). Do you have it? (If you can think of an easier way to explain it on paper, please let me know). Make enough of these wire puzzles for your group. Or, have each set of partners put it together each holding their own paper clip (another activity that might unlock some doors!?)

Now for the game. Partner up players and ask one of the players within each partnership to pick up the interlocking clips. Ask these players to close their eyes. Now ask the other partner, who is sighted, to verbally instruct his/her partner in the steps to take apart the clips. The sighted partners cannot touch any part of the clips or their partner during the game. Also, the clips may not be bent out of their original shape during the game (this is an optional rule). After all the clips are apart switch roles and try again.

POSSIBLE OBJECTIVES:
- Evaluate and develop communication styles.
- Understanding effective directions.
- Giving directions - it's not as easy as we think.

(others)
-
-

Note: I've done this activity two different ways. Do not give the pairs any time to plan, just jump into it and experience the process the first round, each player trying the clips without problem-solving between. After both have had their turn, have the pair discuss and problem-solve, then they each can try it again. The other way I've done it was to discuss and problem-solve after the first player has taken the clips apart before the second player starts. It will depend on the time you have for the activity. The first suggestion takes a bit longer.

The biggest hitch to be aware of is timing. Some pairs finish much earlier than others. Let the pairs talk quietly about their experience or observe others to fill the time.

OBSERVATIONS/QUESTIONS:
- Was this activity easy or difficult?
- What made it easy or difficult?
- Did anyone get frustrated? What was frustrating?
- Did anyone give up on their partner? Why?
- Did any of the unsighted players peek? Why?
- How did you feel when you got the clips apart?
- Who had the more important role during the game?
- Were you able to communicate well with your partner?
- What does good communication involve?
- What did you learn from this activity?

(others)
-
-

VARIATIONS:
- Try this activity without using words. Kids are great at mouth noises.
- I've seen this idea more than once. Before the *Wired* activity, give each participant a paper clip and ask them how many uses they can think of for a paper clip. The idea promotes creative exploration. Looking at things in a different way. Looking outside of the box, etc..
- Put a small puzzle together.

OTHER IDEAS:

STRATEGIC TIC TAC TOE

Thanks to Sam Sikes

NEEDS: You will need a pencil for each player and a few copies of the game grid for each set of players.

PROCEDURE: This activity fits into the competition versus cooperation category. Sam suggests that when you present it to a group, you should give the instructions clearly and quickly before too many questions can be asked. The objective of this activity is for players to try and get as many points as they can. (This will be the key to thinking or working out of the box.)

Split the group into smaller groups of two to four people. Each player in the small group chooses a symbol (shown on the game grid). Like a regular Tic Tac Toe game, players take turns writing a symbol in any empty square on the grid. Again, the objective - players get as many points as they can. Be sure to stop when four like symbols are placed in a row. (Scoring is listed on the game grid and discussed below.)

The idea for the first round or two is never to say they are in competition, but usually they are. Just ask everyone to select a symbol and then emphasize the scoring system, especially that four-in-a-row is four victory points and ends the game.

In subsequent rounds, ask for scores from each set of players and announce the totaled score. Maybe reveal a world record for them to break, like 120 points (actually Sam boasts the record on the 8" x 12" grid of 270 points playing with one other person - they used the same scoring system but found a loophole that I'll let you figure out). You will hopefully see the teamwork lights go off by then if they haven't already.

Scoring is best done after each move. I've provided space under each symbol to keep Tic Marks (pun intended). Let's go over it briefly. Each mark placed on the grid is 1 point for that mark. Three in a row will be 3 points (for the marks) and 2 bonus points totaling 5 points for three in a row. Now keep in mind, you already put down two marks (two points), when you add the third mark to make three in a row you will give yourself 1 point for the new mark and 2 more points for making three in a row. Four in a row, when it's all said and done, is worth 10 points - 5 points you got for the three, 1 point for the new mark and 4 victory points. Then of course the game ends. (You'll have to call Sam if you're lost 'cause I don't think I can explain that again?!)

POSSIBLE **O**BJECTIVES:

- Dealing with the issue of competition.
- Cooperating with others to reach a goal.
- Appropriate peer interactions.

(others)   •

            •

Note: I like this game because it's really easy to set up - most people know how to play Tic Tac Toe. This past knowledge brings up the paradigm of competition, thus playing into my hands. However, it doesn't work as well with groups that know me and the "games" I like to play - so to speak. Anyway, I've had a lot of fun with this one and the groups really seem to get into it.

OBSERVATIONS/**Q**UESTIONS:

- What did you think of the game?
- What was the objective I gave? What was your objective?
- What do you think is important about competition?
- Is there anything wrong with competition? What?
- How did the game change (or not) when you worked together?
- Did working together take away or add something to the game?
- What was it like to be working together toward a goal?
- Did you feel you were successful during the game?
- What did you learn today that you would like to see in this group?

(others)   •

            •

VARIATIONS:

OTHER **I**DEAS:

STRATEGIC TIC TAC TOE

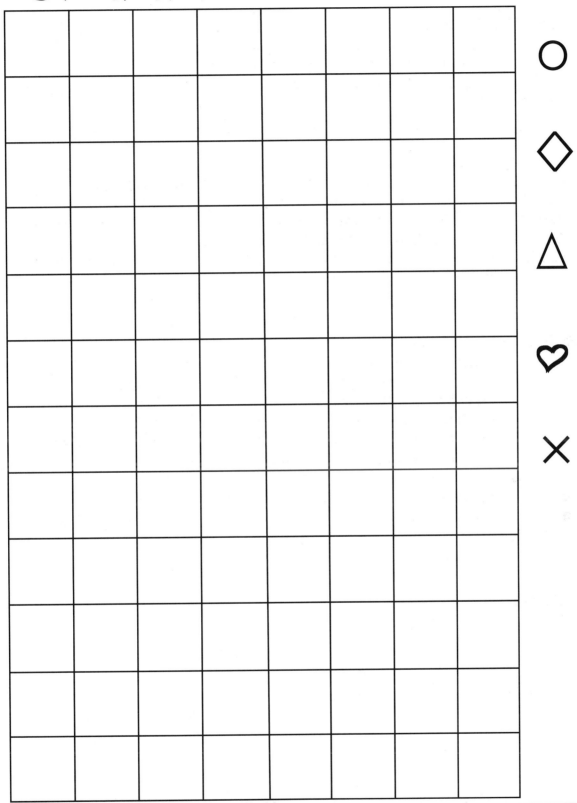

Get into groups of 2 - 5 people. Each person should choose a symbol (just like regular tic tac toe). Take turns writing symbols in any empty square on the grid. Object: see how many points you can score. Stop when 4 like symbols are placed in a row.

Each time a symbol is placed on the grid = 1 point
3 in a row = 2 bonus points
4 in a row = 4 victory points & ends the game

41

THOUGHTS • NOTES • REVELATIONS

NEEDS: You will need a few copies of the game grid. Also, if you can get your hands on an obnoxious buzzer, it adds a bit more anxiety to the process. Vocal BUZZING is necessary if electronic is out of the question. The best place to play *Digital Maze* is on a tabletop or hard floor sitting in a circle.

PROCEDURE: Before this activity you will want to prepare a path through one of the game grids. Start at one of the eight square sides. Place an X in the box that will be the entrance to the pathway. Now place another X in the second row. Continue this process through the rows until you reach the last row of eight. Your X here will be the exit point of the pathway. The more advanced the group, the more complex the maze can be - the more squares you include in the pathway. This grid is now the answer key (that only you can see) to the game.

When the group is ready, give them the blank game grid and explain to them that a secret pattern is hidden within this maze of squares. There is one entrance and one exit. (You will want to indicate which end of the grid has the entrance.) The pattern must be found by walking with the index and middle finger (through the yellow pages), square by square, without skipping any of the squares in the pathway (no passing through walls so to speak). Only one player can touch the maze at a time and players must follow the same "turn" order at all times. A buzzing noise indicates an incorrect square - not marked with an X on the key (I do my vocal buzz if I don't have an electric one). Then the player must exit the EXACT same way he entered or be buzzed again. When a player BUZZES out and exits the maze, he will pass the game grid to the right for the next player. Every time the paper is passed the new player must start from the entrance, not where the last player left off.

After the idea is understood (I hope you get it - if not make it up) tell the group they have five minutes to plan the activity. When they are ready they will need to tell you how many BUZZES they will allow themselves, as a whole group, to get through the pathway. When they have given you their goal and they are ready to start there will be no more talking until the entire group has made it through the pathway or the number of BUZZES has been reached. Basically, no talking during the activity.

If the group exceeds their BUZZ goal, you can choose to continue the game and talk about it later or stop the game, talk about what happened, then regroup for another round. Flip your answer key around so the old exit is now the new entrance. Ready? Go!

POSSIBLE **O**BJECTIVE:

- Learning from failure.
- Peer interaction - pressure, helping, responsibility.
- Planning a task as a group.
- Group goal setting - reaching consensus.

(others)
-
-

Note: The hardest part of facilitating this one is watching the pathway and the group dynamics at the same time. It is really helpful to have another staff member watch the pattern so you can watch the group.

This activity is one of those that may go over the 10-minute window objective of this book, but it is a very interesting one I thought you might find value in. To speed up the process a bit, check the variations below.

One quick word about the goal setting. Setting a goal forces a bit more attention to the process (hopefully) and of course adds some wonderful things to talk about. However, setting a goal of minimum BUZZES is not necessary for a dynamic game. You decide if your group is ready-or-not.

OBSERVATIONS/**Q**UESTIONS:

- How is the five minutes of planning used? Who is the leader?
- What is it like to be BUZZED?
- What kind of help do the players on the grid look for? None? Group?
- Who takes responsibility for the buzzes?
- What is the hardest part about the activity?
- What is important about communication? What type was used?
- What did it take to be successful (taking a risk, failing)?
- Is it hard to accept failure? What if it is needed to be successful?
- How can failure help us?

(others)
-
-

VARIATIONS:
- If you are prepared for anarchy, try this. Change the last square for one person in the group (without telling until you process). This is a great metaphor on discrimination. Some people are not allowed to do what others get to do. This involves risk, so be selective with groups.
- Set a time limit. How will your group work under pressure?
- Letting the group communicate with each other will move the process along a bit faster.

OTHER **I**DEAS:

DIGITAL MAZE

SECTION
Activities using props
TWO

THOUGHTS · NOTES · REVELATIONS

NEEDS: All you need for this one is a canister of plastic monkeys with the arms that hook onto each other. (I'm trying to avoid any copyright laws in repeating the brand name of those monkeys in a barrel?!)

PROCEDURE: Dump out those crazy plastic monkeys on the floor (the floor being my choice of play) and have your group sit around the pile. Choose a starter. (The person with a "z" in there name, the person with only nine toes, or the person who was born in leap-year.) You get the idea. The starter picks up one of the monkeys and following the game rules (the only monkey that can be touched by a person is the first one chosen), picks up another monkey from the pile starting a chain of apes. The pick-up starter, after a successful pick-up, hands the chain of two monkeys to the player on the right. This new player now attempts to pick up another monkey. After a successful pick the picks are passed again to the right. This action continues until all the monkeys have been picked - added to the chain. As they say, "You can pick your nose, and you can pick a monkey, but you can't pick a monkey's nose!" (Sometimes I just can't help myself!)

The only other proviso being, if a picker drops any monkeys off the chain other than the one he/she is trying to pick up at the time, the player must pass the remaining monkeys in the chain to the player on the right and the process continues. This action takes away the success factor for that player for that turn - processing door.

POSSIBLE **O**BJECTIVES:
  • Acceptable peer communications.
  • Establishing encouragement and support.
  • Laughs and giggles.
(others) •
          •

Notes: Please don't underestimate the therapeutic value of *Monkey Business* (pun intended). I have witnessed as much great STUFF emerging from this activity as from any other. I'm finding that the easier the game the easier the door opens (could be a Ph.D. paper?) Besides, this one is great fun too!!

OBSERVATIONS/**Q**UESTIONS:

- What was the initial reaction to this game?
- When was the game easy? When was it harder?
- How did the group support the picker? Positively? Negatively?
- How are we all part of a chain?
- Is a chain harder to form as it gets bigger?
- How can we make the forming easier?
- Was there failure and/or success?
- Are there pros and cons of failure and success?
- What learnings can be pulled from this simple game?

(others)
-
-

VARIATIONS:

- With more advanced groups, have the player on the right verbally instruct a blinded (eyes closed) picker through the pick up.
- Use two sets of monkeys and have a little head-to-head pick-up game. I always find it fascinating to watch what competition does to people. Competition is a valuable attribute if we can compete within the realm of humanity - great topic to dive into!

OTHER **I**DEAS:

CIRCLE-A-LOONS

Adaptation of Karl Rohnke's, Count Down, *Bottomless Bag Again.*

NEEDS: The all out version of this one requires a balloon for each player, but if you can only find one that's all you really need. Keep in mind that if you only have one balloon and it breaks, your game is over! So what am I really saying here? You need a bunch of balloons!

PROCEDURE: You will want to organize your group in a circle. There are a number of circle options here. Sitting on the floor facing center, sitting in chairs facing center, standing in a circle facing the center, or standing in a circle facing front to back with every player's left shoulder directed toward the center of the circle.

When your circle is set, here is the objective: <u>A fully inflated balloon must be passed through the legs of each person in the circle starting and ending with the same person.</u> So let's look at the circle formations we mentioned above. When sitting on the floor, players will have one leg flat on the floor, the other bent at the knee to create a hole for the "loon" to go through. If sitting in a chair a player's feet must be apart in some manner so the loon can pass through. Standing forward would be the same as sitting in a chair - feet have to be apart. When standing front to back, the balloon is passed - football hike style - through the legs.

Seems easy? Let's put the Rohnke challenge to it. "Each person is allowed one-half second for the passage [of the loon] between their legs." Let's do the math. If you have 12 people in your group, they have 6 seconds to get the loon around the circle - starting and ending with the same player. Yes, we are setting the goal for them. We are challenging their abilities. We are dangling a carrot in front of them. We are...... Aren't we? In any case, can they do it? Yes, if they work together.

POSSIBLE OBJECTIVES:
- Cooperation skills.
- Participating within a group.
- Communication skills.

(others)
-
-

Note: I like to include myself in this one if the group can allow me to play without helping them solve any portion of the problem-solving challenges.

I have also used this activity to role-model play-appropriate problem-solving and communication skills. I will go through the S.O.D.A.S. steps for problem solving. Look at the SITUATION we are facing. Discuss possible OPTIONS. Evaluate the DISADVANTAGES and the ADVANTAGES of each option. Finally, choose a SOLUTION we would be willing to try. Somewhat of a long process to learn, but one that becomes more natural with practice.

OBSERVATIONS/QUESTIONS:
- Were you successful? Why? Why not?
- What is cooperation? Was every player cooperating?
- How can cooperating with others help you? Help others?
- Was anyone in the group not cooperating? What was the result?
- How were we communicating during the activity?
- In what ways could we improve our communication?
- What sort of situations did you encounter?
- How were you able to solve the negative situations?
- Was there any leadership taking place? Was it helpful?
- What would you do differently if you were able to try this again?

(others)
-
-

VARIATIONS:
- You might want to let the group determine how long it will take them to get the balloon around the circle. Then you could challenge them with the one-half second each.
- Karl suggests a variation where each player has a balloon with their name on it. Players start with their own balloon. Each balloon must go around the circle back to its original person before the timer stops.
- How about not suggesting any of the circle formation options. Or mention nothing about a circle. Just give them the direction, eliminating the word "circle," and then let the group decide how to solve the problem.

OTHER IDEAS:
If you play the game where every player has their own balloon, Karl suggests that you might want them to take the balloon with them and have them take care of the balloon for a while. Have participants bring their balloon to future sessions checking in on who has their balloon and what such a responsibility had been like. (Remember sex-ed class when you had to take care of an uncooked egg for a few weeks?!)

NEEDS: You're going to need some tower building materials for this one. In the original *Three Towers* activity found in *50 Ways to Use your Noodle* by Sam Sikes and me, we used one of those long foam noodles you can buy in the store - those floaty toys for the pool. The thicker ones are about 58 inches long and 4 inches in diameter (there is also a 3" diameter noodle you could use - Sam and I like the thick ones for building). Then we sliced the noodle up with a serrated bread knife, into 1 1/4" long pieces. You can get a good number of building pieces for just a few bucks. (If you go the noodle route here you can also use them for *Hamburger Press* and *Cup Shapes*.) However, any tower building materials will work, such as wood blocks, Legos® or Lincoln Logs®. You'll want about 30 to 40 building pieces for every four players.

I also like to create a building space for the towers so the group is not moving all over the room (experience is a great teacher). This could be a square of tape, a rope circle, or a hula-hoop with about four square feet of room.

PROCEDURE: The objective for this activity is to build a tower or towers within the building space using all the materials provided. Have the small group(s) sit around their building area. All building materials are placed outside of the area - for now. When the players are ready they will take turns making <u>one</u> of three moves:

1. Add a new piece to the structure from the outside of the building area.
2. Move one piece already within the building area.
3. Move one stack of pieces already in the building area.

There are a few other guidelines. The structure that is being made can only have three points of contact with the building area, So the end result might be three separate towers, two towers, or one big tower with one to three pieces touching the building space. The structure(s) must be able to stand on its/their own and the building must start over when any piece or pieces of the structure(s) fall to the floor.

One other challenge to consider. Will the group be allowed to talk during the construction of the towers or not? Non-verbal activities are so interesting to watch. Maybe one talking and one not?

POSSIBLE **O**BJECTIVE:
- Small group interaction.
- Communication skills.
- Planning and goal setting.

• Compromise development.

(others)   •

                •

Note: This is another great interaction game to watch. If you have more than one group building at a time, it gets a bit challenging to observe all the groups at once. If possible, have someone with you to help observe the groups.

I have had wonderful buy-in for this activity. We all like to build things. Then there are others who like to take apart things. Put the two types together and you have a great deal to talk about!

OBSERVATIONS/**Q**UESTIONS:
   • Was there any pre-planning taking place?
   • Was there any goal setting?
   • What was the result of talking/not talking during the activity?
   • Who was the leader in the group?
   • Was there anything going on between the building groups?
   • What types of non-verbal communication was going on? Was this helpful or not helpful?
   • Did anyone have to compromise their building idea? How did this affect your behavior?
   • How did you feel when someone changed something you just did?
   • Who liked to build? Who liked to take apart? Why?
   • What would your final structure have looked like if you had done it yourself?

(others)   •

                •

VARIATIONS:
   • Pool all the building materials and build the tallest free standing structure. (Interesting leadership interaction here.)
   • Use a variety of building materials together - blocks, foam circles, toilet paper rolls, cups, whatever.

OTHER **I**DEAS:
Get a copy of *50 Ways to Use Your Noodle* for more activities with the noodle slices as well as the longer noodles. (See references.)

— HAMBURGER PRESS

From, *50 Ways to Use Your Noodle*, by Cavert & Sikes.

NEEDS: If you decided to go out and get some foam noodle toys to cut up for *Towers*, (please read the *Towers* activity if you haven't yet) then here's another activity you can do with the foam slices. You need about 30 Meatballs (that's what Sam and I call them), for every couple of players.

FYI. This might not be one of your "official" group activities because you would need a lot of noodle slices. I just thought you might like to use this one if you have a real small group or during those times when a few people are waiting for others to arrive. Plus, it's a challenge!

PROCEDURE: The objective here will be for pairs of players to press as many meatballs as they can together <u>horizontally</u> between their hands.

Dump out all the foam slices you have in a big pile. Working together with another person, each player will use one hand as the press, and the other as an adder. Players start by pressing one of their palms together with their partner. Then, using their adding hands, add one meatball at a time between the pressed hands - making a "hand sandwich." If they want to keep track of slices, they should count as they go 'cause if they lose 'um, all the burgers get mixed up with the others on the floor and there's no way to count them. Be ready for the FFWWAAPP of burgers to occur. What is the FFWWAAPP? You'll see!

POSSIBLE OBJECTIVES:
- Teamwork.
- Goal setting.
- Communication skills.

(others)
-
-

OBSERVATIONS/QUESTIONS:
- How are partners communicating?
- What planning was helpful?
- Was the activity fun? Not fun? What made it that way?
- Are challenges important? Why?
- What challenges are you facing now? Is there anyone that can help you with your challenges?

(others)
-
-

VARIATIONS:
- Have one player feed another player who is pressing the foam slices between his own two hands. How many can one person press?

OTHER **I**DEAS:

I CUP

Thanks to a conference sharing (colleague unknown).

NEEDS: I like to use the small Dixie Cup® for this one - about four for each player. However, if you have collected the number of plastic cups that I have you might have enough for this one. For the "all out" version, you will also need some note cards and a felt tip pen.

PROCEDURE: If you're going to use the "all out" version, you'll need to prepare your cards. Draw the following shapes in order, one shape on each card - Circle, Diamond, Square, & Triangle. You need to make one card for each player - remember, keep them in the above order.

One consideration before you start will be group size. Groups of four to six work the best time wise. You really don't want to go over eight in a group if you have to stretch it. (Family groups are great with this one!) When your group or groups are set, sit them in a comfortable size circle with an open working area in the center of the circle. Hand out one shape card, in order, to each player or (if you don't go the "all out" version), whisper the shape in order, around the circle. The idea here is that each player has one shape to make and players do not know each others' shapes.

Now for the game. Give each player four cups. Players will be taking turns in order. The objective of each player will be to make their shape, with the cups, following the steps below, without talking. If a player is able to make her/his shape, the game will still continue until all the steps have been completed - "without talking."

1. On the first turn each player adds one cup to the working area.
2. On the second turn, each player adds one cup to the working area, and can move one other cup.
3. On the third turn, each player adds a cup and may move two other cups.
4. On the final turn, each player adds one cup and may move three other cups.

When all moves are complete, ask the group members if they can say what shapes the other players were trying to make.

POSSIBLE OBJECTIVES:
- Observation skills.
- Problem-solving.
- Adaptation.

(others)
-
-

Note: This one is similar to the *Towers* activity in this book. Observing behaviors and body language are the keys here. If you have more than one group going, see if you can get some help with observation. You might even want to have one group member sit back and observe what goes on so they can lead some of the facilitation efforts.

OBSERVATIONS/**Q**UESTIONS:
- What was the hardest part of this activity?
- How was the body language during the game? What did it tell you?
- What feelings did you go through during the game?
- Did any player try to influence another player in any way?
- What is adaptation? Did this take place during the game?
- What situations have you had to adapt to lately?
- Were you trying to figure out how to make your shape or were you trying to figure out what the other players shapes were?
- Did anyone try to help another player make their shape?
- Did any players have the same shape? Was there any way to help each other?
- Could you do any planning for your move? What did you have to do?

(others) •
      •

VARIATIONS:
- Give out letters instead of shapes: W, G, R, M.
- Give <u>each player</u> a different shape or letter.
- How about a feeling word?

OTHER **I**DEAS:
Spell, "I CUP." "Why were you lookin!" One of those jokes I played on classmates when I was in second grade. It's funny what we remember!?

NEEDS: You will need a small cloth drawstring stuff sack filled with about six to eight small objects. The objects in the bag should be unique to your specific objectives, and have no sharp edges or corners.

PROCEDURE: The objective for the group will be to guess the contents of the bag without opening it up. The bag is passed once around the group. Players are not allowed to talk, they can only feel the contents from the outside of the bag. Each player is given 30 to 45 seconds for their turn, then they must pass it to the next player.

After everyone has had a turn, make a list within the group of what the contents might be. Everyone has to agree on the items before opening the bag.

POSSIBLE OBJECTIVES:
- Consensus building.
- Opening for topic discussions - relationships, violence, habits.

(others) •

•

Notes: So far you might be wondering how this can be used in a group. What if you put items like a condom or even a rubber O ring that they might think is a condom; a bullet or plastic gun; a pack of cigarettes; a syringe (without the needle); handcuffs. Anything you might want to talk about during a session - your only limit will be safety and size. (Check out Jim and Barry's book, there's a lot more activities you could use.)

OBSERVATIONS/QUESTIONS:
- Which items were familiar to you? (Cain & Jolliff)
- Did you get embarrassed by any of the items? Why?
- Have you ever used any of the items in the bag?
- Did the facial expressions of others alert you to anything unusual in the bag? (Cain & Jolliff)
- What would you put in the bag to talk about?

(others) •

•

VARIATIONS:

- Jim and Barry add that if you've got the time, have two bags ready. The first bag goes around without talking as suggested above. When that process is over, pass the second around and allow discussion as it goes around. (I would add, the first bag could be fun stuff and the second more serious stuff.)

OTHER **I**DEAS:

TABLE-TOP KEY PUNCH

Adapted from Karl Rohnke's Key Punch, *Quicksilver*.

NEEDS: Your main prop here is going to be numbers. There are various ways to present these numbers. The easiest method for getting started will be small paper plates (unused are best). The ones you use for dessert at cookouts after you throw the big paper plates away. You will need 15 small paper plates and a black marker. If you can spare the expense, get the thicker plates so the numbers you write on them won't bleed through to the other side.

PROCEDURE: Write the numbers 1 through 15 on the plates - one number per plate. Make the numbers nice and big so everyone can read them. When your group is sitting around the table or in a big circle on the floor place the plates, numbers down, in random order within the space (table or floor).

Explain to the group that their objective is to decode the number puzzle as fast as possible. How is it done? When the group is ready, the facilitator says, "Go." The players turn over all the plates, keeping them in the same spot, exposing the numbers. Then one player at a time must touch each plate in number-order starting with number 1 and ending with number 15. When the first player has completed, another player counts through the numbers by touching the plates. Each player is allowed one turn to count the plates and no other player is allowed to touch the plates when someone is counting. The last player turns the plates back over (numbers down) in order to end the game. (So, if there is a request for a rematch, just mix up the plates within the area and you're ready to go.)

POSSIBLE **O**BJECTIVES:
- Group interaction.
- Task under pressure.
- Assisting group members in task achievement.

(others) •

•

Notes: If you want to give them time to plan before starting you can. However, most of the groups I have played this with didn't really know how to plan for an activity they had never tried before. If the group wants to try another attempt I give them a chance to plan before starting.

Another point - I don't allow my group members to move from their original spots. This rule brings up interesting conversations about how we see things differently and how it affects performance. This one is full of spine tingling excitement and pressure - what we all thrive on, right?

OBSERVATIONS/QUESTIONS:

- Who gets involved? Why? Why not?
- Why did you participate in this activity? (<u>choosing to</u> is the REAL answer)
- What made the game easier? More difficult?
- How did you help each other achieve the objective?
- Was there any violation of the rules? Why?
- How did your view on/of the situation affect your performance?
- Could there have been anything done to make the activity easier?
- Was it easy to accept help or did you just want to do it on your own?
- Is there any advantage to helping someone?
- What was the end result?

(others) •
  •

VARIATIONS:

- Write numbers on both sides of the plates. Require each player to turn each plate over during his/her turn thus exposing a new pattern every other turn. It's fun to have the little rounded edges on the plates. Some players will have a little easier time picking up the plates than others.
- Use just one sheet of paper and write the numbers in a random pattern on the paper. Players count the numbers down touching each number with their finger, then passing the paper to their right. There is a substantial change in helping each other during this one.
- Ask the group to set an ETC - estimated time of completion. See if they are able to achieve their goal.

OTHER IDEAS:

GUTTER-BALL

Adapted from Lenny Diamond's, *Pipeline*.

NEEDS: You will want to spend a little time saving up some toilet paper rolls, paper towel rolls, and maybe even some wrapping paper rolls for this one. Each player in the group will need one half of one type of roll. Cut the rolls length wise so you end up with two gutter looking props (after cutting you will not have a tube anymore).

You will also need some small wooden marbles - one for each player. These can be found at a craft store that sells all those wood shapes for projects. (If you can't find the wooden marbles check out the variation section below for other ideas.) Also, bring in a few felt tip markers - fine points are best.

PROCEDURE: The objective of the activity is for the group to devise a method for moving the wooden marble(s) through the various hand held pieces of paper gutters and successfully drop the marble(s) into a receptacle located 20 to 50 feet away (depending on the size of the group). Here are the guidelines described by Lenny:

- Gutter pieces cannot touch each other or the ground.
- Gutter pieces may not be altered in any way (no squeezing).
- A player controlling a marble cannot move his/her feet.
- No one can move arms beyond the width of his/her body space.
- Only the first person can touch the marble(s) to get it started.
- Each marble must touch each gutter piece.
- The marbles must not move backward.
- The receptacle cannot be moved.
- Any violation of above guidelines or if a marble drops, it starts over.

Provide the amount of paper gutter pieces you would like the group to use in a big bag or box and let each player choose his or her piece - have a few extras for variety sake - or not! In a small group setting I like to sit in a circle so I can watch the group in action. However, working from one end of the room to the other is just as good. (FYI - if you do the circle, the marbles and receptacle will start out next to each other. To prevent the lateral thinking solution, do not let any player get up from their original position in the circle unless they have to get a dropped marble.)

If you are working with a time constraint, try just a few marbles around the gutters until the group has established some success - or failure. Failure is a good thing if we can learn from it.

If time is not a big factor, try this idea after you pass a few marbles around. Give each player a wooden marble to put their name on. Now put all the marbles at the start. When the lead person picks up a marble to start the action, have him/her call out the name on the marble. "All right, we're sending Mitch around." The marble takes on a little bit more meaning as it goes through the gutters.

POSSIBLE OBJECTIVES:
- Group task - problem-solving.
- Developing communication skills.
- Peer relations.

(others) •

•

Note: As I mentioned above, this one might break the 10 minute barrier depending on the stage of your group's development. I really like the name part of this activity. There are times when you can tell how a person feels about another person in the group by the way they handle a particular marble - respectful, disrespectful, fearful, caring, etc.

OBSERVATIONS/QUESTIONS:
- How did you contribute to the activity?
- What roles were assumed during the activity?
- How did you decide on your gutter pieces? Did everyone get the piece they wanted?
- How was the first person chosen?
- Did anyone else want to be the first person? Why?
- What was the group reaction to dropping a marble?
- What type of problem-solving went on?
- How were the named marbles taken care of? What differences were there?
- How did each person take care of their own marble?
- Could we make this process better? How?
- How can we help each other through the "gutters?"

(others) •

•

VARIATIONS:
- Use anything that will roll down the gutter: glass marble, bead, small rubber ball, BB, gumball into a mouth, egg!?
- More than one piece of gutter per person.
- Place a time limit on the task (one minute from start to finish)
- Non-verbal; one-handed; several members blindfolded.

OTHER **I**DEAS:

THOUGHTS · NOTES · REVELATIONS

HISTORY: I had to add a bit of history to this activity, mainly because I couldn't fit the credit for it in one line under the title. And, because it deserves an historical perspective.

I traced this activity back to the book, *Silver Bullets*, by Karl Rohnke published back in 1984. I'm sure it goes even further back. The activity was/is called, *Mine Field*. Over the years this activity has grown in fame and world wide acclaim as one of the most powerful communication activities to ever see the light of day. Anyway, *Communication Walk* is my name for Danny Williams' *Partner Solve* activity that descended, I'm guessing, from Rohnke's *Mine Field*.

NEEDS: You will want to gather up some blindfolds for half of your group (bandanas work well if you are not dealing with gang issues), and the problem and solution cards from the activity, *P.S.*, found in this book. (If you haven't tried, *P.S.*, please go back and read about the problem and solution cards. You could make up some cards for this game with your group before you play.) Also, if you want the group to develop a running list of comments, supply a small notebook and a pencil for each pair.

PROCEDURE: There are a few ways to set this up, but my favorite is to form a large circle of chairs facing toward the center - three chairs for every two people in the group with a full arm's length between each chair.

Even numbers work best for this one. However, a group of three will work, just rotate accordingly (interesting triangle dynamics). I don't suggest that you play because this one needs someone to "keep their eye on things."

After the circle of chairs is set up, place the problem and solution cards on the floor in random spots, within the circle formed by the chairs. Keep the cards about three feet from any chair.

Partner up group members (you can let them choose partners or you might want to choose for them to observe interaction between two people). Have partners sit in the chairs next to each other. There should be one empty chair between each pair of players. Give one person in each pair a blindfold. Now you're ready for some action.

Before any player puts on a blindfold, explain what will be happening during the activity. One person in the pair will be covering their eyes with the blindfold, this will be the non-sighted partner (NSP). The other partner in the pair will be the sighted partner (SP). The objective of each pair will be for the SP, while sitting in their chair, to guide their NSP to a chair <u>across</u> (no skirting the cards) the circle without the NSP touching any of the cards on the floor. If an NSP touches a card they must take off their blindfold, pick up the card and read what it says to their partner. This problem or solution can be written down on paper (if paper is used) or just remembered. The card is placed back on the floor and the NSP, who can now see, walks back to sit next to their partner (careful not to disturb the cards or the other players). Before playing again the pair must come up with a solution to the problem that was touched or come up with a problem that the solution they touched would work on. Next they write down the response and then switch roles. The NSP becomes the SP and vise versa.

If an NSP is successful in reaching the other side of the circle, the SP should guide the NSP into sitting in an empty chair and then taking off the blindfold. The SP gets up and walks around the <u>outside</u> of the chairs to get the blindfold from their partner, then returns to their original seat to put the blindfold on. The player who made it to the other side will now be the new SP. This SP now tries to guide their NSP across the circle toward the other side (in the direction of the SP). Continue the action of crossing, solving the problems and solutions, and switching roles after each touch until the allotted time is up.

Possible Objectives:

- Communicating directions.
- Listening skills.
- Problem-solving (more ways than one).
- Generate solutions to situations.

(others)
-
-

Note: The main element I keep watch on during this activity is the way SPs are taking care of their NSPs. The trust level of group members, as well as the group, is at stake here. Make sure you stop all inappropriate actions and discuss them with the <u>group</u> before they snowball out of control. On this point, I usually do this activity after the group has been together for a while and has built some trust among themselves.

Keep a special watch for "peekers." If players do not put the blindfold low enough on their face it will be very easy to look down their nose and see the floor. Challenge the players not to peek so each one can experience the full potential of this activity.

Card placement will be another issue to consider. The more cards there are, the less space players will have to maneuver through. So consider the communication abilities of your group before placing the cards. Maybe start out with just a few cards and then start adding cards as the activity progresses. "What happens as additional problems get in our way?"

There will be many challenges that will arise during this one. The most "challenging" will be talking over other players who are talking as well. During all this "fun," SPs have a tendency to disregard or can't see the touches of their NSPs. I often help (I know, but I can't *help* it) notify players of touches so we can generate a good list of problems and solutions and develop that running list of helpful ideas.

If anything else comes up during the game, do a bit of your own problem-solving to figure out what works for your group.

OBSERVATIONS/**Q**UESTIONS:
- What was the greatest challenge of the activity?
- Were you able to work through this challenge? How?
- Did you follow all the rules? Did anyone peek?
- Did any pair establish any special way to communicate?
- What were some of the problems you encountered? What were the solutions you thought of?
- What were some of the solutions you encountered? What were some of the problems these solutions could help with?
- What do you encounter more of in life, problems or solutions? Why do you think this is the case?
- Where could you go to find solutions?
- What sort of trust was involved in this activity?
- Did anyone lose or gain trust during this activity?
- What does it take to build trust within a group?

(others)
-
-

VARIATIONS:
- If you have the time or you are working with a small group, send just one player blindfolded across the circle and have the group try to guide this person over. If there is a touch, talk about the problem or solution and then switch players.

69

• Use just "problem" cards in the circle. Generate a list of possible solutions.

OTHER **I**DEAS:

— TABLE TOP BULL RING —

Thanks to Jim Cain and Barry Jolliff, *Teamwork & Teamplay.*

NEEDS: You will need one Bull Ring (described below) for every 12 players and a variety of magnet things, cones, marbles and other small objects that can move around on the surface of a large table at the center of the group - so you're going to need one large table and one chair for each player.

So what is a Bull Ring? You're going to have to bear with me as I explain this - don't give up because this one is grand!! A Bull Ring consists of a metal ring 2 inches in diameter (or pretty close to it) with thin strings radiating outward. As some of my groups would say, "It looks like the sun with rays of light coming out." This metal ring can be found at most local hardware stores in the fastener section. (Jim says you can also use a large diameter key ring to do the job). I also buy my string at the hardware store (it saves me another trip). I use the thin synthetic cord that comes in bright colors. Really, any thin strong string will work. When making a Bull Ring for a group of 12, cut six pieces of string 20 feet long and tie each end so the tips don't fray - if you're using synthetic you can also burn the tips a little after you tie them. Take the string and fold it in half. Place the metal ring inside the bend at the halfway point in the string, then tie the string to the ring with an overhand knot - that first part of tying your shoes two times. Do this with each of the strings. You now have a Bull Ring -12 separate strings (10 ft. long) radiating from a central metal ring. Now, after all that, you can play.

PROCEDURE: The challenge of this activity is to capture the various objects, scattered about on the table, with the metal portion of the Bull Ring and move them to a designated collection place located near the edge of the table.

Before the group comes in for their session, set the metal ring in the center of the table and then lay out the strings around the table so they drape over the edges of the table. Set a chair back from each overhanging string. Once you have this sunshine set-up, place the items that you're going to move on the table between the rays of sunshine. Here are some of the items Jim and Barry have tried: refrigerator magnets, magnet marbles, cone shaped items, marbles, a crumpled piece of paper, a suction cup dart stuck to the table, a brand new pencil, a paper clip, and a piece of duct tape (but I'm not sure how you get it unstuck from the table? - I haven't tried using the tape yet). Ready!?

As your group arrives, have them choose a chair and ask them not to touch anything (a challenge in itself for many of our young friends!) When everyone is ready you'll want to start the activity with players holding the midpoint of each string. This allows everyone to release and pull without losing their connection with the group. Inform the players about moving the objects to the designated holding bin (I tape a piece of paper down near an edge) keeping these guidelines in mind:

1. The string may not touch or move any object on the table unless the part of the string touching the object is also touching the metal of the ring.

2. Players are not allowed to touch any of the objects with any body part until the object is within the holding area.

3. Players must remain in their seats until all objects are moved into the holding area.

4. All players must have a hold on their string until all moving is completed without wrapping the string or tying it to any part of their bodies.

And there you have it - I hope? Have Fun!!

POSSIBLE OBJECTIVES:
- Communication within a group.
- Introduce and develop "Task vs. Maintenance" understanding.
- Develop effective communication skills.

(others) •

•

Note: It will be <u>very</u> important not to let participants tie or wrap the string around their fingers or wrist. This action could cut off circulation or cause rope burn during sudden movements.

Keep in mind, the more items you have, the more time the activity will take. You can also save time by placing one item on the table at a time so players do not have to worry about touching one object while moving another.

I have used this activity to discuss the concept of "Task and Maintenance". The "Task" being the project at hand and the "Maintenance" being the care and consideration of group members. During any group project the group should try to achieve a balance of each so all needs are met and the task gets done in a reasonable amount of time. During Bull Ring, notice how much attention is focused on the moving object - the task, and how little attention is given to effective communication and needs assessment of the players involved - the maintenance. So much to talk about. "What's good for the group is good for the gathered." (I just made that up, what do you think?)

OBSERVATIONS/QUESTIONS:
- What was the initial reaction to the activity?
- Was there any planning involved?
- Did your group have a strategy for which items to retrieve first? (Cain & Jolliff)
- Did the strategy change as time went on? Was it abandoned? Why?
- Which objects were the easiest/hardest to acquire? (Cain & Jolliff)
- Describe some of the communication that was going on during the activity. What would you change about it?
- Where was the focus of attention during the activity? What was the group worried about the most?
- What are some things that are important to remember when working within a group of people?
- What would each group member like from the group when working together? What do you need, to feel as though you're part of the group?
- Was there any leadership in the group?
- How did the leadership help or hinder the progress?

(others) •
    •

VARIATIONS:
- Build your Bull Ring with a rubber band instead of a metal ring!?
- Attach a wide-tipped marker to the center of the ring with (lots of) masking tape. Then challenge your group to write something on a piece of paper that is taped to the table.
- Pick up a copy of *Teamwork & Teamplay,* for other great ideas.

OTHER IDEAS:

OTHER IDEAS FOR TABLE TOP BULL RING:

SECTION THREE

"What would it be like" ...

THOUGHTS · NOTES · REVELATIONS

...to have a whole bunch more questions that started with, "What would it be like?" (I'm assuming you have already used some from the first Games for Group). You're not sure? Well here is your chance to find out. The list that follows can be integrated into group session, transition times, or just sitting around. Anytime you have some time.

The following questions are presented in closed format. This means they can be answered with one word (usually a feeling word in this case). It is your choice as a facilitator to expand on the questions if you think the individual is ready to do so and you have the time. Sometimes it is better to let one word answers be enough. This can build trust for future discussions.

If you would like to expand on the questions, here's the idea: "What would it be like to write your own biography?" Answers could vary from, "not interested" to, "exciting, I could get the movie rights." Expanding on the responses is also wide open. It will be up to you as the facilitator to take it in the direction that looks open. "What would be some of the chapters in your book?" or "Who would be some of the other characters." Then expand upon those answers. You get the idea.

There are a couple of ways that I have presented these questions. I've just opened the book and said, "Who would like to pick a number?" This makes the atmosphere relaxed and non-threatening. At other times I planned ahead and picked questions that relate to a certain group discussion that I wanted to have. Both ways have worked well.

Be careful not to spend too much time with one person. I will always allow the option to pass or choose a new question. (I usually don't allow more than one chance to pick another question - time problems). If the question seems to cause reaction with others, open the question up to the group. (I usually set up guidelines to prevent others from answering someone else's question or blurting out an answer). Use your time evenly among the group members to keep the interest going.

Don't forget to take a turn yourself. It is a good way to become part of the group. Have fun with the questions so you'll leave them wanting more! Maybe pick the last question of the session like, "What would it be like to create your own dessert?" Oh, and if you're wondering why the questions start with number 205 - Games (& other stuff) for Group has the first 204 questions. (See the resources section in the back for information on how to get a copy. Also, I have to plug another great resource. If you like the "question" type format check out, "The Me I See: Life Questions for Teens," by Wood & Barnes Publishing Staff. It's a journaling book with 400 questions in it. See resources section for examples, pgs. 104-108.)

Have fun! And if your group wants to make up more questions, send them to the publisher for inclusion in the next, Games for Group!!

What would it be like...

205. to reach the top of the highest mountain?

206. to be bitten by an animal?

207. to swim on the back of a whale?

208. to be taller?

209. to have no thumbs?

210. to discover a new species of animal?

211. to discover a cure for AIDS?

212. to hike for a week in Antarctica?

213. to attend a summer sports camp?

214. to go to a space camp?

215. to attend a computer camp?

216. to be lost in the mountains?

217. to have your face on money?

218. to have a statue made of you?

219. to have a building named after you?

220. to hold a black belt in a martial art?

221. to live to be 100?

222. to be a missionary worker?

223. to be a model?

224. to be a lawyer?

225. to go deep sea fishing?

226. to write your own biography?

227. to grow up on an army base?

228. to ride over a waterfall in a kayak?

229. to drive a tank?

230. to be the taste tester for the Jelly Belly® company?

231. to watch a baby being born?

232. to be a baggage handler at an airport?

233. if you could only eat once a day?

234. to work in a cookie store?

235. if you had no hair?

236. to spend a week with _____ ? (pick a person)

237. if you were drafted?

What would it be like...

238. to move in with your grandparents?

239. if you couldn't taste anything?

240. to go snowmobiling?

241. to be a roadie for your favorite band?

242. if you only had one leg?

243. to stay overnight on the street?

244. to breath underwater?

245. to stay overnight in an airport?

246. if you saved a baby bird that fell out of its nest?

247. to discover a new planet with other living beings?

248. if you didn't have ears?

249. to go base jumping? (parachute off a cliff)

250. to ride in a glider?

251. to lose all that you own in a tornado?

252. to have a flat tire?

253. if we all had the same color skin?

254. to never have to study, and get all A's?

255. to be robbed?

256. to invent a game?

257. to change one of your facial features?

258. to live in a teepee?

259. to witness a crime?

260. to go to military school?

261. to be the number one skateboarder in the world?

262. to be a taxi driver in a big city?

263. to ride in an open air bi-plane?

264. to lose your wallet?

265. to travel in a submarine?

266. to have a clone of yourself?

267. snowbound in a cabin?

268. to ride a motorcycle across the United States?

269. if your best friend told one of your secrets?

270. not to have any form of government?

What would it be like...

271. if someone said you were beautiful/handsome?
272. if you could trade places with one of your family members?
273. to own a jet ski?
274. to be the director of a movie?
275. to own a television station?
276. to be in a different family?
277. to be a magician?
278. to have a butler?
279. to be a butler/maid?
280. to be a chauffeur?
281. to be a professional golfer?
282. to dress up as Santa Claus?
283. to receive a diamond ring?
284. to be an orphan?
285. to be a therapist?
286. to work at a fast food restaurant?
287. to bag groceries for a living?
288. as a pizza delivery person?
289. to have your own Web site?
290. to own a beach front condo?
291. to have a beeper?
292. to invent a new form a transportation?
293. to shave your legs?
294. to shoot an animal?
295. as a famous artist?
296. to be in the Peace Corps?
297. to help with Habitat for Humanity?
298. to be an active member of Green Peace?
299. to have your own charge card?
300. to be a nurse?
301. to go snowboarding?
302. to snow ski in Colorado?
303. spending a week on a houseboat?

What would it be like...

304. in Vegas?

305. traveling around the country in a mobile home?

306. to get fired from a job?

307. to be voted the Most Valuable on a sports team?

308. to design your own amusement park?

309. to camp out in the snow?

310. to be a pro tennis player?

311. if someone asked you for your autograph?

312. to be the world's fastest human?

314. to receive a dozen roses?

315. to raise your own farm animals?

316. to fire a machine gun?

317. to win a trophy?

318. to go paintballing?

319. to be in love?

320. to work on an oil rig?

321. if there were no laws?

322. to spend a day in the city of your choice?

323. to be color-blind?

324. if the weather was always 72 degrees and sunny?

325. to go to the Hawaiian Islands?

326. if you could not communicate with others for a week?

327. to appear in a commercial?

328. if you informed the police of a friend's crime?

329. to win a lottery?

330. to be a zoo animal?

331. to take back one bad thing you did?

332. to have anything in the world for one day?

333. to carry a casket?

334. to change any one rule?

335. to be a stunt person?

336. to wear braces on your teeth?

337. if you could bring one person back to life?

What would it be like...

338. if someone offered you green eggs and ham?

339. if everyone you knew had a surprise birthday party for you?

340. to get a pie in your face?

341. if you could have any job you wanted?

342. to be the only one home watching a scary movie?

343. to become allergic to your favorite food?

344. if you were chosen to live in a biosphere for one year?

345. to miss your high school graduation?

346. to be on a sinking ship?

347. to travel on a yacht?

348. to teach a class of your peers something you're good at?

349. if you had a secret safe?

350. to have a bodyguard?

351. to have a best friend?

352. to be without a telephone?

353. to build your own tree house?

354. to have stitches in your body?

355. to make a movie of your life?

356. to wear a tie every day?

357. to win an Oscar?

358. to be the only survivor of a plane crash?

359. not to eat for a week?

360. if you couldn't listen to any music for one year?

361. to host a late night talk-show?

362. to do community service work for an elderly residence home?

363. to live in an elderly residence home?

364. to get up every morning for work at five o'clock?

365. if someone wrote a song about you?

366. to drive a car in a demolition derby?

367. if you created a new sport?

368. to encounter a bear?

369. to call any one person on the phone and talk for one hour?

370. to collect baseball cards?

What would it be like...

371. to milk a cow?

372. to shovel out a horse stable?

373. to ride in a rodeo?

374. to have a new first name?

375. to be a private detective?

376. to leave your body to science?

377. to be an All-Star Wrestler?

378. to dissect a frog?

379. to dissect a human body?

380. to summit Mt. Everest?

381. to walk through walls?

382. to eliminate one subject from school?

383. to be a radio D.J.?

384. if drugs were legal?

385. if you were charged for a crime you didn't commit?

386. to be a camera man for action news?

387. to drive through the mud in a monster truck?

388. if you could communicate with animals?

389. to be Miss America/Mr. Universe?

390. to wake up and be a different race?

391. to wake up and be purple?

392. to stay overnight in a penthouse suite?

393. to find a winning lottery ticket with a name on it?

394. to discover a car with the keys in it?

395. to be a dentist?

396. to have your own apartment?

397. to work on a cruise ship?

398. to be mistaken for a celebrity?

399. to lose all your teeth?

400. to go cliff diving?

401. to be a garbage man?

402. to drive an armored car?

403. to be a house cat?

What would it be like...

404. to be a school bus driver?

405. to clean other people's houses for a living?

406. if you discovered a genie in a bottle?

407. to spend the night in a haunted house?

408. to be without a watch?

409. to rent out a movie theater for one night?

410. to set a world record?

411. to be a substitute teacher?

412. to visit a morgue?

413. if you could see in the dark without special equipment?

414. to rescue someone from a fire?

415. to eat $10 worth of McDonalds®?

416. to sing the Star Spangled Banner before a sporting event?

417. to know the day of your death?

418. to be the main headline of tomorrow's USA Today®?

419. to create a new hot-dog?

420. to have parents of a different race than you?

421. to have private use of a mountain resort for a week?

422. if you never needed any sleep?

423. if all electronic games were banned?

424. to have an all expenses paid, month-long trip?

425. to live in a castle?

426. to design your own neon light?

427. if you were stranded on an island by yourself?

428. if you didn't make any mistakes?

429. to live in a house with no running water?

430. to be a catholic priest?

431. to create your own candy bar?

432. to choose between curtain #1 and a thousand dollar bill?

433. to be a master chess player?

434. to be a secret agent?

435. to get rid of your biggest fear?

436. to be a superhero?

What would it be like...

437. to be in a world without flowers?

438. to be without flush toilets?

439. to receive a large package in the mail?

440. to stand in a line for 45 minutes?

441. to ride a train across America?

442. to add any one thing to your surroundings?

443. to have your own business card?

444. to visit with your favorite sports star?

445. to be stuck in an elevator?

446. to be a guest on your favorite television show?

447. to go on a cattle drive?

448. to own a restaurant?

449. to own 10 acres of land?

450. to go on a jungle safari?

451. if you had to move every two years?

452. to have a lifetime subscription to your favorite magazine?

453. to have your picture on the cover of a magazine?

454. if you won $10,000 but you had to give it all away?

455. to have a mohawk haircut?

456. to make ice-cream by hand?

457. to go ballroom dancing?

458. if you got held back a year in school?

459. if someone proposed to you?

460. to jump into open ice water? (polar bear club)

461. to get a tattoo?

462. to go ice climbing?

463. to wear the same clothes every day?

464. to be divorced?

465. to body surf waves over 8-feet tall?

466. to be buried in the sand up to your neck?

467. to be in a world without deodorant?

468. if we ALL had hairy armpits?

What would it be like...

469. to start a fire without matches?

470. to climb 50 feet up into a tree?

471. to fall out of a tree?

472. to have your own Fan Club?

473. to go on a blind date?

474. to work at a library?

475. to see a live, active volcano?

476. to go skinny dipping?

477. posing nude for an art class?

478. if you couldn't read?

479. to be an angel?

480. to live in a Waterworld? (like the movie)

481. to be fluent in all languages?

482. to be a mermaid/merman?

483. to be alive inside another person?

484. to know everyone in the world?

485. to be extremely underweight?

486. not to know your parents?

487. if the sun was blue?

488. if the world was black and white?

489. to never be embarrassed?

490. if there was no pizza?

491. if we didn't have cats?

492. if money grew on trees?

493. if there were no mirrors?

494. to kiss a movie star?

495. to live on airplanes?

496. to be the Vice-President?

497. to live like the Jetsons?

498. to be caught in a tornado?

499. to live in a cartoon?

500. to feel no pain?

What would it be like...

501. to be liquid?

502. to be loved unconditionally?

503. to feel no happiness?

504. to journey to the center of the earth?

505. to be loved by everyone?

506. if you could not smell?

507. to be lost in a foreign country?

508. if you never wore underwear?

509. if you got stood up at your wedding?

510. to be an elephant trainer?

511. to read people's minds?

512. to be an orchestra conductor?

513. to walk on water?

514. to press a button that launched an atomic weapon?

515. to wear dentures?

516. to eat every meal with your hands?

517. to have temporary amnesia?

518. to go to a nude beach?

519. if there were no more tests?

520. if your hair turned gray over night?

521. to never hug anyone?

522. to never get a hug from anyone?

523. to grow up with wolves?

524. to have cars with wings?

525. to own a solar-powered car?

526. if you kissed someone and they turned into a frog?

527. to speak singing every day?

What would it be like...

Submit your ideas of more "What would it be like..." for our next publication to Mony Cunningham, Wood 'N' Barnes Publishing, 2717 NW 50th, OKC, OK 73112

SECTION FOUR

Metaphors

THOUGHTS • NOTES • REVELATIONS

I have been using metaphors as a tool for a long time and I didn't even realize it. One day I was working with a group doing what is called the *Human Knot*. Everyone is attached at the hands and the arms are all jumbled up. The objective is to untangle the arms and end in a human circle. From the center of the human mass I heard, "I don't think we're going to unscramble this omelet!" These same words were used the day before in a debriefing about getting into trouble and how difficult it is to set things right again. It occurred to me, at that moment, that metaphors are another tool to add to one's box. From that day on I started putting together a list of helpful metaphors:

- For communicating advice and warning in different situations: "Be careful not to run in blindly." "Don't blow your top."
- For promoting creative thinking in participants: "All roads lead to Rome." "How could we bend the rules a little to solve this problem?"
- For developing a common language between group members: "I'll go to bat for you." "Don't rock the boat or we might get into trouble."
- For learning different ways to look at the world: "Let's break some new ground." "A bird in the hand is worth two in the bush."

The deeper meaning in such simple phrases can go a long way in a short time. The brain is activated when it hears, "Isn't that the pot calling the kettle black." It has to stop and think (we hope). Then evaluate. If we just say, "You do that too," the defenses come up, "I do not," and the brain stops working.

So, how else can you use metaphors with a purpose? Start topical conversations. Say you want to talk about rules. If you just jumped in and said, "We're going to talk about rules today." You might not get a real open-minded attitude in the room. What if you said, "Does anyone know what 'grin and bear it' means?" Discuss the metaphor to find out what sort of things they have learned to 'grin and bear.' Then after the group realizes they have already obtained the skills to 'grin and bear', why not 'grin and bear' the <u>rules</u>? The back door approach - but it can work.

Use metaphors as signals. Arrange an agreement with a group member or with the entire group, that when you use a certain metaphor the person or group will try to stop and evaluate the situation they are in. Say you use, "You might not want to burn any bridges today." This could signal the need to stop and look for behaviors that might be causing bad feelings and hopefully change those to more positive ones.

Use metaphors with the activity, *Mix and Match*, in this book. It adds some problem-solving that can take the group into a learning moment. What more could you ask for? I'm sure you can find many ways to use these tidbits of philosophy to engage the minds of your groups.

The following collection of metaphors are general in scope. I encourage you to adapt or add to these to make them culturally appropriate for the group you're working with. Engaging the brain is what we all strive for. If we always use the same words, we will most likely get the same responses. I hope this "Metaphors for Life" section will open some new doors.

OTHER IDEAS:

Metaphors for Life:

1. Break the ice.
Start a conversation or discussion.

2. Don't add fuel to the fire.
Don't do or say anything that might make the situation any worse.

3. Let's not leave it up in the air.
Let's try to finish what we started.

4. Let's brainstorm.
To collectively work together to come up with new ideas.

5. It will all come out in the wash.
The facts of the issue will all come out in time.

6. I'm all ears.
I am ready to listen to what you have to say.

7. Don't run into a blind alley.
Take on the situation slowly and carefully so you can see any problems that might be ahead.

8. We seem to be up in arms.
A level of excitement that might lead to a harmful outcome.

9. Ask and you shall find Rome.
You have a better chance of getting what you want if you ask for it.

10. No strings attached.
A willingness to do something for someone without expecting anything in return.

11. When the cat's away the mice will play.
Without appropriate supervision there is a tendency to get into trouble.

12. Backseat driver.
A person who is looking to gain control over one who is in control.

13. Don't look a gift horse in the mouth.
If you're given something for free, don't complain about it.

14. Going to bat for someone.
A willingness to take on a task for someone who is unable to, or sticking up for someone.

Metaphors for Life:

15. Zero in.
Move toward a desired goal.

16. You live in the house you build.
Accepting the consequences of one's actions.

17. Sailing under false colors.
To pretend that you believe or support something when you really don't.

18. Bend the rules.
To overlook minor rule violations, or changing the rules to fit one's needs.

19. Set the wheels in motion.
To take action, or get things started.

20. The early bird catches the worm.
To take advantage of a good opportunity before others do.

21. The sand is running out.
The time allotted for a particular situation is almost over.

22. Bite your lip.
To hold back your anger, or to hold back words you want to say in order to keep the peace.

23. Beauty is in the eye of the beholder.
We are all entitled to our own opinions.

24. Opening Pandora's box.
To start trouble that will affect many others.

25. Let's get down to brass tacks.
To talk about the facts that really matter.

26. Get your act together.
Organize what it is that you are doing so that you can be helpful to the group.

27. Break new ground.
Attempt to do something you never have before.

Metaphors for Life:

28. I wasn't born yesterday.
Having more knowledge and understanding of a situation than others give a person credit for.

29. Water under the bridge.
A situation that is in the past and is no longer relevant.

30. Clean up your act.
Change a negative behavior into a more positive one.

31. Burning bridges.
Deliberately doing something that will end or drastically change a relationship or situation from that point on.

32. Wipe the slate clean.
Forgive someone for something done in the past.

33. Every cloud has a silver lining.
There is something to learn from even the worst experiences.

34. Up to your armpits.
To be very involved in one thing or very busy doing several things at once.

35. Nail your colors to the mast.
To make others aware of your belief in something and stand up for it no matter what.

36. Come in out of the cold.
To be welcomed into a group of people.

37. We'll cross that bridge when we get to it.
Not to worry about tomorrow's problems today, because there might not be any problems tomorrow.

38. Painting yourself into a corner.
Getting one's self in an undesirable situation that will be difficult to get out of.

39. A loose cannon on deck.
A situation or person who is close to trouble or about to get out of control.

40. Spill the beans.
Telling the truth about something that happened.

Metaphors for Life:

41. Still waters run deep.
If a person is quiet, it doesn't mean he/she does not possess great knowledge.

42. A diamond in the rough.
Good qualities on the inside that are covered up by negative behaviors.

43. Watch the doughnut, not the hole.
Look at what you have instead of what you don't have.

44. There are many ways to cook an egg.
There is more than one way to do something.

45. To each his own.
Every person has the right to do things their own way.

46. Let's put it to bed.
Finish a project or get rid of something once and for all.

47. Don't judge a book by its cover.
Don't assume some characteristic or quality in someone based on the way they look.

48. Don't bite the hand that feeds you.
To be disrespectful to a person or persons who physically takes care of you.

49. Get off the fence.
Choose an option or side of an issue that is presented.

50. Where there's smoke there's fire.
If there is some suspicion of trouble, then it is likely that there is trouble.

51. Get in the game.
Participating by the rules in what is happening.

52. Don't rock the boat.
Don't do anything that will disturb a peaceful situation.

53. Speaking with a forked tongue.
To tell another person misleading information so the truth is not discovered.

54. Put your best foot forward.
To give your best effort, or show your true talents.

Metaphors for Life:

55. People in glass houses shouldn't throw stones.
You should not make fun or criticize someone when you have the same quality or characteristic.

56. Sitting on your hands.
Taking no action during an event or situation.

57. Let you hair down.
Take it easy or relax.

58. Going behind someone's back.
Doing something that one was told not to do and attempting to hide it.

59. You can't put the genie back in the bottle.
It is impossible to undo something that just took place.

60. Caught between a rock and a hard place.
To be forced to choose between two undesirable choices.

61. Getting out of hand.
A situation is becoming unruly or out of control.

62. Beat the odds.
To succeed even though you were expected not to.

63. Stir up a hornet's nest.
Get involved in something that may turn into an unpleasant situation.

64. Bury your head in the sand.
To not accept the consequences of an immediate situation.

65. Just the tip of the iceberg.
There is more to the situation or problem than appears.

66. Let's keep the ball rolling.
Continue doing what is going on at that moment.

67. Jumping in feet first.
Taking a risk that one believes will be of benefit.

68. Speaking the same language.
All individuals involved understand what is going on.

Metaphors for Life:

69. Turning over a new leaf.
To change your current way of doing things to another way that may have a more positive outcome.

70. Hiding your light under a barrel.
Not revealing one's talents and skills.

71. The grass is always greener on the other side of the hill.
It appears that another situation - where one has no experience - is better than the one they're in.

72. Keep your fences mended.
Do not leave problems unresolved.

73. Some mud is going to stick.
Accusations discovered to be untrue will still leave harmful side effects.

74. Mind over matter.
Gaining a better chance of succeeding by making a conscious decision to overcome an obstacle.

75. You can't make an omelet without breaking eggs.
To achieve a desired goal you might have to go through some hard times.

76. On task.
Doing or saying things that are related to the issue or situation at hand.

77. Pass the buck.
Pass the responsibility for something on to someone else.

78. Look outside of the box.
Look for an answer that is different than the obvious one.

79. Paying lip service.
You can say the words but do not perform the action. (You know the rules but do not follow them.)

80. You're not the only fish in the sea.
There are other people in the same situation that you are in.

81. Pull out all the stops.
Give the maximum effort to a situation.

Metaphors for Life:

82. Read between the lines.
To understand something not put into words.

83. Throw your hat into the ring.
Speak up about a position that interests you.

84. Fiddling while Rome is burning.
Avoiding the main issue while discussing irrelevant events.

85. Learning the ropes.
Learning the basic rules of a group or situation.

86. Biting off more than you can chew.
Taking on something you will be unable to accomplish.

87. On the same page.
All parties involved understand what is going on.

88. Make hay while the sun shines.
Take the opportunity to do something before it disappears.

89. To bare your soul.
Be very honest about how you feel inside.

90. Let sleeping dogs lie.
Don't bring up past issues which are not relevant.

91. Take the good with the bad.
Accept the difficult parts so you can experience the pleasant ones.

92. Starting from square one.
Starting over without being subject to past circumstances.

93. Grin and bear it.
Accepting an uncomfortable situation without complaining.

94. You can't unscramble an omelet.
It is impossible to take back words spoken or an event that occurred.

95. A bird in the hand is worth two in the bush.
Having something in your possession is better than expecting something you may never get.

Metaphors for Life:

96. The writing on the wall.
To accept a future situation as fact.

97. Breaking down the barriers.
Reconsidering a belief that is possibly preventing a positive solution to a situation.

98. The wrong wavelength.
A misunderstanding between people.

99. Up against a brick wall.
Unable to accomplish something due to the lack of help from others.

100. An old head on young shoulders.
A young person who possesses the maturity of an older person.

Submit your ideas of more "Metaphors for Life" for our next publication to: Mony Cunningham, Wood 'N' Barnes Publishing, 2717 NW 50th, OKC, OK 73112

Metaphors for Life:

Submit your ideas of more "Metaphors for Life" for our next publication to: Mony Cunningham, Wood 'N' Barnes Publishing, 2717 NW 50th, OKC, OK 73112

Metaphors for Life:

Submit your ideas of more "Metaphors for Life" for our next publication to: Mony Cunningham, Wood 'N' Barnes Publishing, 2717 NW 50th, OKC, OK 73112

References & Resources

Cain, J., & Jolliff, B. (1998). *Teamwork & Teamplay*. Dubuque, Iowa: Kendall/Hunt Publishing. (800) 228-0810.

Canfield, J. & Self-Esteem Seminars. (1985). *Self-Esteem in the classroom: Seminar Manual*. Culver City, CA.

Cavert, C. (1995). *E.A.G.E.R. Curriculum: Experiential activities, games, and educational recreation*. Oklahoma City, Oklahoma: Wood 'N' Barnes Publishing. (800) 678-0621.

Cavert, C., & Sikes, S. (1997). *50 ways to use your noodle: Loads of land games with foam noodle toys*. Tulsa, Oklahoma: Learning Unlimited. (888) 622-4203.

Nadler, R. S. & Luckner, J. L. (1997). *Processing the adventure experience: Theory and practice*. Dubuque, Iowa: Kendall/Hunt Publishing. (800) 228-0810.

Renton, N. E. (1990). *Metaphorically speaking: A dictionary or 3,800 picturesque idiomatic expressions*. New York: Warner Books.

Rohnke, K. E. (1996). *Funn stuff*. Vol. 1. Dubuque, Iowa: Kendall/Hunt Publishing. (800) 228-0810.

Rohnke, K. E. (1994). *The bottomless bag again*. Dubuque, Iowa: Kendall/Hunt Publishing. (800) 228-0810.

Rohnke, K., & Butler, S. (1995). *Quicksilver: Adventure games, initiative problems, trust activities, and a guide to effective leadership*. Dubuque, Iowa: Kendall/Hunt Publishing. (800) 228-0810.

Schoel, J., Prouty, D. & Radcliffe, P. (1988). *Islands of healing: A guide to adventure based counseling*. Hamilton, MA: Project Adventure. (800) 796-9917. Also, ask for their training and equipment catalogs.

Sikes, S., & The Activity Colloquium. (1997). *Just for fun*. Unpublished document. (888) 622-4203.

Sikes, S. (1995). *Feeding the zircon gorilla: And other team building activities*. Tulsa, Oklahoma: Learning Unlimited. (888) 622-4203.

Staff of Wood 'N' Barnes Publishing (1998). *The Me I See: Life Questions for Teens*, Oklahoma City, Oklahoma: Wood 'N' Barnes Publishing. (800) 678-0621. (This book is a personal journal with 400 questions and tons of space to write - aimed primarily for teenagers.)

If my life was a MOVIE, this is who would be in the credits & what their job was...

☆ Starring?

Co-starring?

Directors?

Cast?

Crew?

Producer?

Music?

Script?

Catering by

85. The relative who has made the greatest impact on my life is...   because...

86. This is what people say or do that can make me really angry...

87. These are some boundaries I try to set in my relation-ships...

I love to...

88. These are my thoughts on living together before marriage...

345. *things that* **keep** *me* AWAKE *at* **night** *are...*

346. my **favorite** *is...* **fairy tale** *because...*

347. When *my* **parents** *are* **angry** *with* me, they...

348. The **people** *I am most* **comfortable** **around** *are... because...*

Sample pages from <u>The Me I See: Life Questions for Teens</u> (referenced on page 77)

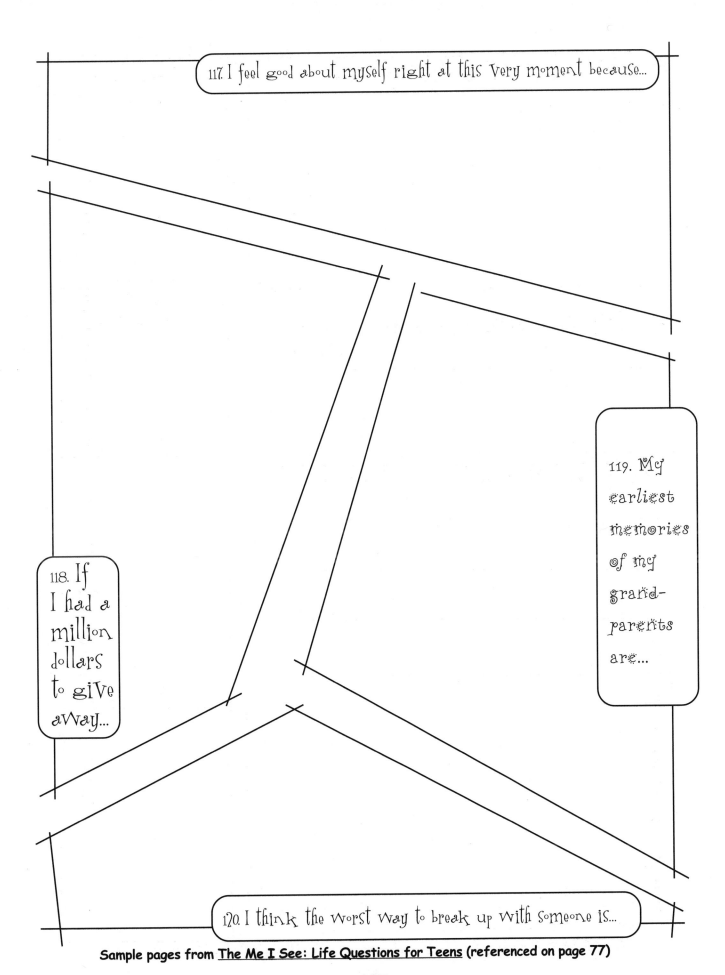

117. I feel good about myself right at this very moment because...

118. If I had a million dollars to give away...

119. My earliest memories of my grandparents are...

120. I think the worst way to break up with someone is...

Sample pages from <u>The Me I See: Life Questions for Teens</u> (referenced on page 77)

337. This is how I am like my father...

338. **My favorite day** of the week is...
because...

_____

_____

My favorite time of day is... because...

_____

_____

339. If I could live anywhere in the world for the remainder of my life, it would be... because...

340. These are the feelings that are the hardest for me to express... & this is how I deal with them...

Sample pages from The Me I See: Life Questions for Teens (referenced on page 77)

Order Form

To order copies of Chris' books or any of the resource books/games referred to in this book you may use the following form:

JEAN BARNES BOOKS, 2717 NW 50th, OKC, OK 73112
or you may call us at 405-946-0621 or 800-678-0621

Please enclose payment with your order and add $4.50 for shipping and handling plus $.75 for each additional book/game ordered. Books will be sent via United Parcel Service. Mastercard, Visa, Discover and American Express accepted. Oklahoma residents please add 7.375% sales tax.

NAME _____

ADDRESS _____

CITY/STATE _____ ZIP _____

CREDIT CARD # _____

EXP. _____ TELEPHONE # (____) _____

SIGNATURE _____

QTY	AUTHOR	TITLE	PRICE

Subtotal   _____

Sales Tax   _____
(OK - 7.375%)

Shipping   _____
& handling

($.75 for each   _____
addl book)

TOTAL   _____

JEAN BARNES BOOKS • 2717 NW 50th • OKC, OK 73112
ph 405-946-0621 • ph 800-678-0621 • fax 405-946-4074
e mail - jean@barnesbooks.com • website - http://www.barnesbooks.com

THOUGHTS · NOTES · REVELATIONS

THAT'S ALL FOR NOW